UNSTUCK!

*Seven Easy Steps to Break Free and
Get Back on Course to Living in B.L.I.S.S.!*

Valerie Brunnberg

*Valerie Brunnberg
International*

UNSTUCK! Testimonials

If you are feeling stagnant in your life, this book will be the catalyst to get you *UNSTUCK!* Valerie Brunnberg so gracefully leads us down the path of possibility toward our ultimate destiny. Her seven-step process shows how the smallest steps create the momentum needed to move you into purpose and a life you were meant for. Like a mother nurturing a child, her step-by-step process allows us to grow through each phase of our journey with all the love and support we will need.
—Audra Erwin, "High on Life Coach," www.audraerwin.com

Brilliant Read! Valerie Brunnberg opens up her heart and soul in her first book, *UNSTUCK!* She takes you through life's peaks and valleys, with a dash of faith, to uncover what might be holding you back from living your bliss. This book will inspire, motivate, and give you practical how-tos to conquer self-doubt and become an unstoppable force! *UNSTUCK!* is a must read for anyone who's ready to fulfill their passion and purpose but needs a guide to lead the way.
—Lynn Bardowski, speaker, consultant, and author of *Success Secrets of a Million Dollar Party Girl*, http://milliondollarpartygirl.com

Valerie Brunnberg has a brilliant way of weaving real-life stories with inspirational quotes and "right here, right now" steps that will help her readers get *UNSTUCK!* and start thriving in their lives again!
—Janie Lidey, Emmy Award–winning songwriter, speaker, author, and artist, Alaskan Angel Productions, www.janielidey.com

Beautifully written and divinely guided, *UNSTUCK!* will inspire you as you read Valerie Brunnberg's story of losing her zest and meaning for life. But even more, it will liberate you beyond measure as you apply the very same steps she discovered that led her to a life of profound meaning, exhilarating joy, and multifaceted abundance. *UNSTUCK!* is not just a treat to read; it is divine wisdom that works.
—Maryann Ehmann, speaker, coach, and author of *Create Your Magnificent Life Now*, http://maryannehmann.com

I love how the B.L.I.S.S. Points Map touches every aspect of our lives. Brunnberg's interactive book asks the questions that really encourage you to dig deep, set, and visualize your true B.L.I.S.S.! Then "exercise your consistency muscle" to create your true happiness and a legacy to leave behind. This book is a must read for anyone feeling depleted, overwhelmed, and stuck!
—April Iannazzone, speaker, coach, leader, and founder of Florida Women Business Owners, www.3sSuite.com

Published by RockStar Publishing House

Copyright © 2015 Valerie Brunnberg International

All rights reserved. No part of this book may be reproduced or transmitted in any form or by any means, electronic or mechanical, including photocopying, recording, or by any information storage and retrieval system without written permission of the publisher, except for the inclusion of brief quotations in a review.

Printed in the United States of America

Brunnberg, Valerie
UNSTUCK! / by Valerie Brunnberg
ISBN: 978-1-93750-684-1

The purpose of this book is to educate and entertain. Neither the author nor the publisher guarantees that anyone following the tips, techniques, suggestions, ideas, or strategies will become successful. The author and publisher are in no way liable for any misuse of the material.

Cover design by: Gary Wein

Layout by: Scribe Inc., Philadelphia, PA

Photos by: Dawn Burke and Warren Goldswain

"For every positive change you make in your life, something also changes for the better. It creates a chain reaction."
—Leon Brown

Contents

Foreword by Yvonne Oswald, PhD	ix
Acknowledgments	xiii

Introduction	1
Shock My Soul: The Cocktail Party That Started It All	3
Step 1 Use Today	7
• Make the Decision to Get Unstuck	7
• Start with Baby Steps	9
• Prepare for the Climb	15
Step 2 Navigate Your Course	17
• Get Clear on Your "Why"	17
• Have Faith	19
• Picture Yourself Living in B.L.I.S.S.	21
• Turn on Your Possibility Thinking	23
• Expect Detours	27
Step 3 Start Making Yourself More Visible	31
• Show Up	31
• Speak Up	33
• Step Up	34
Step 4 Train Your Thoughts	39
• Watch What You're Thinking	39
• Choose Your Words	41
• Change Your Story	43
Step 5 Unleash Your Passion	47
• Ask Questions to Spark Your Passion	47
• Plug Yourself in and Get Reenergized	49

	• Sharpen Your Senses to Increase Your Blessings	52
	• Turn Your Passion into Action	54
Step 6 Celebrate Something Each Day		57
	• Celebrate YOU	57
	• Celebrate by Being Grateful	58
	• Celebrate by Activating Your Endorphins	60
	• Celebrate by Playing	61
	• Celebrate by Giving	61
	• Celebrate the Little Things	62
Step 7 Keep Your Commitments		65
	• Make a List	66
	• Keep Your Commitment to God	68
	• Keep Your Commitment to Others	68
	• Keep Your Commitment to Yourself	70

Afterword	73
Appendix	75
Notes	77
Recommended Resources	81

Foreword

Yvonne Oswald, PhD

Sometimes seemingly insignificant events can have a profound impact on one's life. Valerie Brunnberg's awakening came at a party that had a theme of "Come as you will be," as she realized that she had become frozen in a closed loop of unhappiness of her own making. And yes, we've all been there! And then we ask ourselves how it happened: how did we get caught up in that neutral loop of inaction that seems, by all appearances, to have no way out? In hindsight, we can often look back and see a simple solution that would have taken us to a happier and faster ending if we had had more information or simply made a different choice at that time.

In *UNSTUCK!*, Valerie Brunnberg, a speaker, trainer, and one of the most dynamic and powerful woman leaders I know, takes you on a journey to freedom in seven clear, easy steps that allow you to bridge the gap between perception and reality and identify simple strategies to open up new and better choices, taking you to that blissful state of inner harmony and happiness. Happiness is an elusive state that mankind has been seeking for thousands of years. Everyone wants to find it and live in it, although the actual meaning of the word is multifaceted in its various contexts. Is happiness something that can be found, or is it something that can be engineered, or does it arrive naturally once negative emotions and nonsupportive decisions are released? Can it be regulated to appear daily by conscious learning?

Living with stress and anxiety has become the prevalent practice of life in 21st-century America, and one thing is certain: happiness and stress cannot live comfortably in the same world. Stress is another word for needs unfulfilled, or deficit needs, as Maslow referred to them. Although humans are a most uniquely adaptable species, emotional emphasis seems to have been on coping or dealing with the aftereffects of stress on the mind and body rather than on attending to finding daily happiness. Valerie Brunnberg has put together a book full of wisdom and practical ways to break free from the gray zone of inaction and immobility and get moving along the path to inner freedom and outward abundance. She offers amazingly insightful and easy ways to open up and make small, fast changes through conscious intent, leading to success and self-actualization by tapping into hitherto undiscovered inner treasures.

The result is not, as was at first thought, living a life in the sun with endless bliss as a companion but rather traveling a road of consciousness leading to what Greek philosopher Aristotle called *eudaimonia*—flourishing in a whole world of dedication to purpose, experiencing the now in all its fullness, and enjoying fulfilling and rewarding relationships through kind collaboration. It is connecting to life, intelligence, love, laughter, and grace in the pleasurable expectation that emotions will rise and fall and always trusting that the deep inner self of conscious connection will remain eternal like a flame of warmth and strength inside.

I wish for you the most amazing life: a life where every day you wake up thrilled to be alive and happy to be here; a life where you live and walk and think in sunshine, in happiness and joy, full of self-love and a sense of completeness and fulfillment; a life where you explore and take chances, a life of prosperity, health, love, self-acceptance, empathy, and success beyond your wildest dreams. You live in a house that is comfortable and beautiful, you eat healthily, and you have a wonderful family and warm friends. You travel, give back, and enjoy the excitement of living in gratitude of a deeply fulfilling, strong life full of purpose. You stay true to yourself on every level as you love learning, growing, and passing on knowledge to make others' journeys to joy sweeter and shorter.

Awakening is a process. I believe that the most important lesson to learn in life is that you have to be the light in your own world before you can be the light in others'. As a trainer of hypnosis and neuro-linguistic programming (NLP), it is with delight that I was able to be a part of Valerie's rise to success. Her thirst for knowledge and her application to self-growth are a delight to someone like me, who lives and breathes to meet and train people who will step up to the plate, stand alongside me, and change the world. Follow Valerie as she guides you, always one or two steps ahead of you, leading you forward on your life's journey with ease and grace. To shorten that journey to joy for others is one of the most powerful things anyone can accomplish.

It starts with you. Destiny is calling. It's time to own it and move forward. Deepen your experience of life as you read on. It's time to find your own shining light. . . .

Acknowledgments

> "We cannot swing up a rope that is attached only to our own belt."
> —William Ernest Hocking

I must first thank God for the abundant blessings in my life, for leading me on this wonderful journey, and for coauthoring this book with me. To Craig Duswalt, thank you for your guidance and inspiration. I'd like to thank Dr. Yvonne Oswald who taught me how to train my thoughts and switch my language to produce greater results in my life. Thank you also for mentoring me on bringing this book to life. I'd like to thank my amazing friends who have been instrumental on my journey to getting **UNSTUCK** (there are too many to name ... you know who you are). Special thanks to Donna Knox, one of my greatest supporters, thanks for always being there when I needed you. I'd like to thank my family, my brothers and sisters, and my extended family. Thank you for your love, support, and friendship. My special thanks goes to my sisters: Susanna, for inspiring me to run and teaching me a few tricks of the trade when I was getting started, and Jenny, for being my sounding board on this journey and for providing me with such sage advice over the years. I love you both! To my beautiful mom (my very first best friend), thank you for raising me with such unconditional love and helping shape me into the woman I am today. I love you! To my angels in heaven—especially my Dad, Grandma, Grandpa, and Matthew—thank you for watching over me. To my husband, Tom, you have transformed my life in countless ways! Thank you for being my partner, my soul mate, and best friend. You have stuck by me in the good times and in the not-so-good times; whether I was stuck or **UNSTUCK**, you remained by my side! I love you forever and ever!

Introduction

> "Some people die at 25 and aren't buried until 75."
> —Benjamin Franklin

There was a time in my life when I thought I had *arrived*. I had risen to the top level within my company. I was making more money than I ever thought possible. I was fit, happy, and healthy. I had overcome my greatest fears (or so I thought), and my confidence level had soared to new heights. I was very happily married and blessed with great relationships with my family, friends, neighbors, and coworkers. I was **UNSTUCK**.

But slowly over the years, something changed. Little by little, inertia crept in and established residence in my soul. It was as though I woke up one day and was living a stranger's life. I no longer recognized myself. I had gone from fit to fat, from financially thriving to just surviving, and from creating the life that I wanted to merely accepting whatever life dished out. I had stopped taking care of myself and, frankly, I had just quit caring . . . period. I was living in the physical sense. I just no longer felt alive. **And then it happened.**

Like a defibrillator to my soul, an odd incident shocked my spirit back to life. An invitation to a simple cocktail party (and what occurred at the event) awoke a sleeping giant and kick-started my journey of rediscovery and renewal. I am excited to share with you the details of how my spirit was awakened and the steps I took afterward.

Chances are, because you're reading this book, you know how it feels to be stuck. You may have asked yourself questions like "How did I get here? How did I end up like this? What happened?" Or even, "**WHEN** did this happen?"

What I've realized is that life tends to enjoy throwing us an occasional curveball. It was on my own journey of getting **UNSTUCK** that I uncovered seven easy steps that would help me break free and put me back on course to living in **B.L.I.S.S.** (*Because Life Is So Spectacular*). If you find yourself stuck, I invite you to use the ideas in this book to get moving in the right direction again. It is my wish that these same seven easy steps will assist you in breaking free and will get you back on course to living in **B.L.I.S.S.** again too.

Shock My Soul

The Cocktail Party That Started It All

Long before the cocktail party, I had been searching for myself, looking for my passion, and trying to rediscover my purpose. I didn't know what I wanted out of life or which direction I wanted to take. I just knew that something had to give.

My zest for living had disappeared. Physically, I had grown lethargic. My entire adult life, I was able to stay a women's size 6 with relative ease. Then, in my 40s, I went from a 6 to an 8 and then to a 10. And before I knew it, I was a 12 and inching toward the next size up. I decided it was menopause and thought that it was just a sign of aging.

My home-based business that was once fun and easily generated a six-figure income had taken a financial downturn and simultaneously became more like a job. I figured it was the economy.

I had lost my confidence and became more fearful of stepping outside of my comfort zone. I often wondered, *Why can't I just be satisfied with what I have and where I am in life? Why do I feel the need to strive for more?* And that little voice inside my head kept urging, *Stay inside your comfort zone where it's safe. Surely you can be happy here.*

One of the ironic things about all this is that from the outside looking in, most people would wonder what it was I was searching for. I was very happily married to a great man, and together we had a wonderful life. We went on great vacations, had a nice house, drove nice cars, and lived in a nice neighborhood. Still, for me, something was missing. At times, I felt guilty for not being satisfied. There were plenty of people in the world who were way less fortunate than me and *they* seemed to be happy. What was happening to me? I felt . . . almost . . . broken.

I wanted to fix it and I looked everywhere for answers. I attended conferences, seminars, and webinars; listened online to various programs; read books . . . I longed to figure out the link that seemed to be gone from my life.

Then I got an invitation to a cocktail party. It was a "come as you will be in five years" party.[1] We were told to bring props and be prepared to converse and "act as if"[2] we were the person that we wanted to be five years from today. It was suggested that we bring fake awards, trophies, certificates—whatever props we wanted that would show what we had accomplished. *What on earth am I going to do now?* I thought to myself. *I have been trying to figure out my future for the last three years! Now I've got two days to have it all mapped out! Maybe I just won't go.*

I called my baby sister to share my feelings and ask for some guidance, as we've always been great sounding boards for each other. She suggested I go as an inspirational speaker. Over the years, I had developed a passion for speaking. I had spoken to audiences from 10 to 10,000 and had even shared the stage with Jack Canfield, the world-renowned coauthor of the Chicken Soup for the Soul series. Yet, at this time in my life, that woman seemed like another person to me, and I now lacked the confidence to imagine giving a speech to an audience of any size.

I hung up the phone still not knowing what I was going to do, and I continued running my errands. But over the course of the next several hours, thoughts started to flood my brain about who I was going to be in five years. It was as though the universe was sending me signals. By the end of the day, I had it all figured out. By midnight, my props were ready to show off to all the attendees. For the first time in a long time, I began to feel alive! As I drifted off to sleep, I felt a great sense of peace mixed with an excited anticipation about what my future and the next night's cocktail party held in store for me.

* * *

I entered the dimly lit room where candlelight flickered softly on tall cocktail rounds draped with black tablecloths. Along the back wall, long tables held chafing dishes filled with appetizers, their sweet aroma infusing the air and beckoning the guests to come and take a peek. There was a soft buzz of quiet conversation as guests mixed and mingled. Servers offered up glasses of champagne from a tray, and I politely accepted as I scanned the room hoping to see someone I might know.

Most of my life, I had been quite an extrovert. I could command a great presence and be very entertaining—"the life of the party," as they say. That part of me had also gone into hiding. Now I found myself feeling awkward in this room filled with strangers. Part of me just wanted to retreat, except for the fact that if I did, I wouldn't get to show off my wonderful props, which I had stayed up until midnight creating. I spotted a group of friendly looking ladies and decided to go and introduce myself and see if I could join their table.

Throughout the evening, everyone was making small talk. Not a soul was "acting as if." No one mentioned any props. Nobody said a thing about the theme of the party. At one point, one of the facilitators of the event got on the microphone. I thought, *OK great! **Now** she'll get the party started. Surely she will remind everyone of the theme and that it was time to "act as if."* But nothing was mentioned. I was confused. *Did I just dream the party had a theme?*

I mustered up the courage to start the conversation with the ladies at my table. "Did any of you bring props tonight?" I asked.

"Props? What are you talking about?" questioned one of the women.

"She's talking about that email we got the other night," said another.

"Email? What email?"

"It was sent out late Wednesday night. They wanted to make this a 'come as you will be party,' with everyone bringing props and awards representing what you had done in the next five years. It was a last-minute idea, and the email was sent out late, so not everyone got it. I saw it but didn't have time to do anything about it."

As it turned out, not a single person at that party had prepared anything! Not one person was ready to "act as if," *except for me*. At the end of the evening as the cocktail party concluded, I headed to my hotel room for the night, and I thought to myself, *WOW! I did all that work for nothing!*

Almost immediately, I heard a little voice inside my head whispering, *"No, my dear . . . not for **nothing**. You did that work for **everything**! You did that work to get **UNSTUCK!**"* It was as though that party theme was added just for me—the universe's way of getting me to begin figuring things out and bringing me back on course to living in **B.L.I.S.S.**

> *"Coincidences mean you're on the right path."*
> —Simon Van Booy

STEP 1

*U*se Today

"Everyone who got where he is had to begin where he was."
—Robert Louis Stevenson

Make the Decision to Get UNSTUCK

As I already said, for years I had wanted to get back on the right path. I had a strong desire to figure out where I was going and what my future would hold. I wanted to lead a life of passion and purpose again. The difference between wanting something to happen and making something happen lies in the **decision** to bring that want into reality.

The word *decision* is formed from the Latin root *cis*. And *cis* originates from a Latin root that means *"cut"*. The word *incision* means *"to cut into,"* whereas the word *decision* means *"to cut off."*[3]

When you make a decision, you cut off all other possibilities that anything will happen outside of the result on which you have decided. When you decide, you are committed to that end result. The very first step on your own **UNSTUCK** journey is to **USE TODAY** and *make the decision* that *you will get back on course to living in B.L.I.S.S.*

Imagine getting that same invitation and the cocktail party is two days from right now. Envision people at that party that you've always wanted to meet—your heroes, idols, and people you highly respect and look up to. This is a party that you have a strong desire to attend, and you now will figure out what props to bring with you. You will decide who it is that you will be five years from today. Getting **UNSTUCK** will be a short step from now.

USE TODAY to make the decision that you've been stuck long enough. It's time to change right now, and you're ready and willing to do whatever it takes . . . to take any necessary steps that will get you back on top again and to enjoy life as God intended you to enjoy it—to be alive and truly ***THRIVE! USE TODAY and MAKE THE DECISION. It's really an easy first step.***

You may want to start by asking yourself these questions:

- Am I ready to get **UNSTUCK**?
- Am I ready to start thriving in my life again?
- Am I ready to experience great success?
- Am I ready to enjoy life, have fun, and reap the rewards of abundant living?
- Am I ready to be happy and to truly feel happiness deep down within my soul?
- Am I ready to start putting myself out there again?
- Am I ready to step outside of my comfort zone?

- Am I ready to make some changes, no matter how uncomfortable they may feel, knowing that *the rewards lie just on the other side* of that uncomfortable feeling?

USE TODAY and make the decision to say yes to those questions. For those of you who still may have a small voice inside that sometimes wants to stay the same, get ready *to step out in faith* and begin *to move forward once again*. We will talk more about how to handle that little voice in Step 4, "Train Your Thoughts." For now, just be clear and tell that little voice, *"I've got this! I can handle it from here! We're moving full speed ahead and getting back on course to living in B.L.I.S.S.!"*

> *"When someone makes a decision, he is really diving into a strong current that will carry him to places he had never dreamed of when he first made the decision."*
> —Paulo Coelho, *The Alchemist*

Are you ready to journey with me to exciting new places which already house your very own unexplored fabulousness? ***Let's go!***

Start with Baby Steps

> *"The journey of a thousand miles begins with a single step."*
> —Lao-tzu, Chinese philosopher

One of the fastest ways to begin getting **UNSTUCK** is to simply get moving in any area of your life in very small ways! The thought of getting that new job, letting go of excess pounds, getting your house organized, becoming financially free, and so on can seem so overwhelming that procrastination can occur. The way to release that habit now is to **USE TODAY** to take a first step. Then just take a small step every day to *exercise your consistency muscle*. Doing small things on a consistent, daily basis prevents the feeling of being overwhelmed and can add up to one big victory. *Overnight success* happens when the *accumulation* of all the days of *preparation* actually become *THE* big break.

So you might be asking yourself, *"How do I take a step when I don't yet know where I am going?"* Baby steps are **less about direction** and **more about movement**. If you've ever watched a baby learning how to walk, you know that at first, the baby is just learning how to use those legs. Once the baby gets the hang of it though, she is ready to move with ease to achieve her goals! She now knows how to get to where she's going—that cookie on the table; that pretty, shiny object on a shelf; and so on. You are kind of like a baby that just needs to learn how to use her legs. The first thing you want to do is to just start to take action again. We will talk about how to "Navigate Your Course" in Step 2, so for now, you just want to get mobile.

How does that look, sound, and feel? It's different for everyone and it depends on how deep the *stuckness* is (yes, I made up that word). Let me just share a few examples of getting mobile again. You might want to simply go for a walk for just five minutes a day and be conscious of the beautiful outdoors, inhaling that fresh air and just noticing nature. Allow your spirit to get in tune with the quiet surroundings. You might enjoy taking a class that sounds like fun to you, such as photography, computers, yoga, sign language, dancing, golfing, swimming, painting, singing, playing a musical instrument, cooking, jewelry making, and so on. You could choose to pick up a basketball and learn to dribble or just shoot a few hoops. Perhaps you'd like to grab a jump rope or a Hula-Hoop and see how long you could go without stopping. Another idea might be to find some paper and a pen, pencil, or crayon—whatever you prefer—and just start drawing. It could even be playing in the rain, jumping in mud puddles, or running barefoot through the grass.

These were the little things that made our spirit come alive when we were kids. And as an adult, these activities can once again bring a new sense of harmony to you. By getting mobile in this way, you will help your soul feel energized and enthusiastic again. Doing one or more of these activities will prepare you so that once you are ready to navigate your course, your spirit will dive right into the journey ahead of you.

For me, one of my baby steps was to take up running. After getting a good pair of running shoes and socks, it was easy to get started and I could practice it at any hour of the day, so I could fit it into my schedule. I could just get outside and go. This was important for me because it cleared any excuses I might have had.

Once I decided I was going to start running, I realized that I needed a goal: something that I could work toward. What was it that I would be running for?

I *did* have a half marathon on my life list, and so I decided to search for *half marathons* on the Internet. When I found the Disney Princess half marathon, I was so excited. The tag line was something like, *for any little girl who grew up to be a woman wanting to make her dreams come true.* It simply spoke to me, and I registered right away to complete the 13.1-mile course.

Having never run anything longer than three miles (and even that was 20-plus years prior), I now believe that it was God who was guiding my steps all along the way. I didn't recognize it at that time, but looking back, there is no other explanation for how I thought I could accomplish this task on my own without having any training.

About seven weeks later, among more than 20,000 other runners, I crossed the finish line and earned my first half-marathon finisher's medal. That was just enough to get my soul singing again. It would eventually lead me to many more half marathons and also to my next business: one that would make my spirit soar and allow me the opportunity to give back to the world in a big way.

Never underestimate the power of taking baby steps! Let me take some time to share with you how profound your baby steps can turn out to be!

I never would have dreamed that by taking up running, it would lead me down the path I am on today. Ten months after I first laced up, I discovered the world of virtual races. Two months after that, I organized my very first virtual race as a means to raise funds for my team in the American Cancer Society's "Relay for Life" event.

A virtual race is one where you register online (FitFabAndLean.com), download your customizable race bib, and choose your own course (indoors on a treadmill, outside in your neighborhood, on a track around a cruise ship while on vacation, or pretty much anywhere on the planet). When you're ready, you simply put your race bib in a page protector and pin it to your workout clothes. Then you complete the miles on your own time. Once you finish and report your results, you're awarded with a finisher's medal in celebration of your achievement.

Virtual races give you the flexibility to fit a workout into your schedule while also giving you the accountability to stay the course and be consistent in your efforts of staying physically active. A virtual race is for anyone who has a desire to improve his or her physical fitness, even if he or she has never run before. You can walk the miles, run the miles, or do a combination of the two. There are also races where you can bike the miles, swim the miles, or complete them on a step or elliptical machine. And you can complete the miles all at once or you can split up the race over a period of days or weeks. Within our virtual racing organization, Fit, Fab & Lean®, one of our mantras is "Crawl until you can walk. Walk until you can run. And then run and inspire others to do the same." It's not about breaking records. It's about being consistent so that you develop the habit of maintaining a physically active lifestyle.

The first virtual race I organized was a big success and was so rewarding to me that I decided to turn it into a fun, little side business where I could earn income and also give back to the community. Though my virtual-racing business is a for-profit organization, charity plays a huge role in my life and is one of the biggest motivating factors of my career. I believe one of the greatest rewards of being financially secure is having the ability to give to others. As I am writing this book, our company has been able to donate tens of thousands of dollars to various causes based on the success of each of our virtual events.

That one little virtual race that I first organized in February of 2013 has turned into the development of Fit, Fab & Lean®, Inc.—a global organization whose mission is to empower women to step into their **B.L.I.S.S.** through fitness while also bringing awareness and financial gains to charitable causes. We have participants from all over the world and we are changing lives as a community.

All of this is what it is today because of the baby step I took when I bought a pair of running shoes and running socks and decided to complete my first half marathon.

Speaking of baby steps, do you know how I began writing this book? By writing the first sentence. Do you know how I began writing the first sentence? By writing the first word. Did that word or that sentence change along the way? Sure! That's the beauty of being able to edit. But the key was *I GOT STARTED!*

As you begin, I want you to understand that you won't always know where your baby steps might take you. You just have to **USE TODAY**, take that step in faith, and get moving.

In his 2005 commencement speech at Stanford University, Steve Jobs called this "connecting the dots" and said, "You can't connect the dots moving forward. You can only connect the dots looking back." One of Steve Jobs' own baby steps was to take a calligraphy course. He attributes that step to being the reason today "that computers have the beautiful typography that they do."[4] Had he not taken that course, who knows what would have happened? It could have possibly changed the whole trajectory of technology.

I hope that at this point you are beginning to feel excited about the possibilities that lie ahead for you and for your future! I hope that you can see that by starting small, you could end up doing something quite grand. The path of **B.L.I.S.S.** that I am currently enjoying began with baby steps. Start with baby steps and you can produce sweet success too.

> *"Remember to dream big, think long-term and take baby steps. That is the key to long-term success."*
> —Robert Kiyosaki

What baby steps will you begin to take now so that you too can achieve long-term success? How will you **USE TODAY** to start "getting mobile" again? What sounds like fun to you? Write down whatever comes to mind.

_____
_____
_____
_____
_____
_____

What is ONE THING you can begin doing today, and continue doing tomorrow, and the day after that, and the day after that, in order to develop your consistency muscle that can eventually lead you to your dreams? Decide what that step will be and *write it down*.

One baby step I can take today is _____

_____

_____

_____

And then be like Nike and . . . *"Just Do It"!*

Prepare for the Climb

> *"The person who removes a mountain begins*
> *by carrying away small stones."*
> —Chinese proverb

Once you've learned how to *use your legs*, so to speak, it will then be time to prepare to climb that proverbial mountain. Come up from the valley, climb back up to that peak, and enjoy the view from the summit.

Looking back on my **UNSTUCK** journey, I now realize that in life, there will always be peaks and valleys. Although we may love the view from the top, there are different reasons for descending into the valley. Someone once said, "We are meant to climb mountains not so that **THE WORLD** can see **US**, but so that **WE** can see **THE WORLD**."

Sometimes when we get off track, God leads us back down the mountain to regain perspective. In the valley, there is a well of humbleness, gratitude, understanding, love, and compassion. When we are in the valley, we must fill up our reservoir to prepare for the climb back up to the peak.

Another reason one descends into the valley is to go back and find others who might need some assistance. We take them by the hand, lead them to the well to fill up their own reservoir for the journey, and then we guide them up the mountain as we climb together.

I mention these reasons for descending into the valley because I want you to understand that when you find yourself there, it doesn't mean that you have to stay there. So fill up your reservoir and get going once again!

Once your reservoir is full and you're ready to ascend, that mountain can still appear pretty immense. That is why we want to look at the path in front of us and just start taking steps. As Martin Luther King Jr. reminded us, *"Take the first step in faith. You don't have to see the whole staircase, just take the first step."*

So **USE TODAY** and make the decision to get started. Stand up and take that first step in faith. Remember that, for now, it's more about movement than direction and just get mobile. After all, there is no need to adjust the sails when you're still at the dock. It is only when you've left the harbor and your boat begins to catch the wind that you will then course correct so you're moving in the direction of your destination.

Fill up your reservoir by continuing to feed your mind with the kind of thoughts and ideas that move you forward on your journey. Read great books (like this one) and listen to audio recordings that will continue to inspire you to scale that mountain. Do something every day, even if it's just picking up this book again and rereading a chapter. For at this stage of your journey, it's not so much the **SIZE** of the action that you're taking as it is the fact that **YOU ARE TAKING ACTION TODAY**!

> *"Realize deeply that the present moment is all you ever have."*
> —Eckhart Tolle

STEP 2

Navigate Your Course

"Divide it into small jobs."
—Henry Ford

Get Clear on Your "Why"

As the saying goes, "Know how to eat an elephant? One bite at a time." You've got to take your big goals and break them down into bite-size pieces. Know how to get to where you want to go? By starting with *WHY* you want to take the journey to begin with. Think of your *WHY* as the fuel your car will need to get you to your destination. To clearly define your *WHY*, I recommend that you create your **Bliss Points Map**. As I mentioned earlier, **B.L.I.S.S.** is my acronym for *"Because Life Is So Spectacular,"* and when you're following your **Bliss Points Map**, it truly is!

We'll get to your map in a while, but first, let me share a little background with you. When I first started reading self-improvement books and attending self-improvement courses, the buzzword back then was *balance*. Everyone talked about living a life in balance. The thing about balance, though, is that if you've ever looked at a scale that is balanced, the same amount of weight is on the left side as is on the right! And guess what? The scale is not moving. If you maintain that, it is, in essence, stuck. It's not going anywhere. True life has an ebb and flow. It is fluid and so it is constantly moving. Think of it as two kids playing on a seesaw. One pushes off the ground with her feet to send her upward and then the opposite child pushes off the ground and does the same. To keep moving forward in life, you want to alternate between giving energy and receiving energy. When your life is moving and fluid and you are giving and receiving energy, it means that oxygen is flowing, blood is pumping, and the heart is working. That is when you truly feel alive!

The **Bliss Points Map** is made up of ***four hearts, which are grounded in faith***, represented by the cross in the center. Take a look at the following diagram.

One heart represents relationships and friends and family, one heart represents health and leisure, one heart represents money and career, and one heart represents leaving a legacy.

In medicine, a pulse is taken to measure how well the heart is working. When taking a pulse, you're counting the heart's *beats per minute* (**bpm**). With your **Bliss Points Map** (**BPM**), you'll be measuring how well each heart is working in order to analyze how healthy you are for the journey toward a blissful life. It's not about spending an *equal* or *balanced* amount of time in each heart because each heart requires a different level of focus at different times. Each day, you'll simply measure how well you believe each heart is beating. Ask yourself, *"In which B.L.I.S.S. point would it be most favorable for me to dedicate some time this week?"* and then write down some action steps you can take that will keep that B.L.I.S.S. point beating strong.

Have Faith

Before we dive into the four hearts, let's start with the cross in the center, which represents God/faith. For some of you, this part might be easy. And for others, this might be a challenge. Those who find it challenging may not be sure about God, and some may feel like they never knew God to begin with. I know how that feels because I have felt the same way. And what I have found is that when we just keep the doors of communication open to possibilities, wonderful things can begin to happen.

Looking back on my journey, I realize that during those times when I had found myself grounded in faith, the blood was flowing and the oxygen was pumping so that all four hearts were beating strong and providing me with optimal health in all aspects of my life. Take away that cross and squeeze those hearts together and the life flow slows down. I believe my own peaks and valleys could have a direct correlation with the presence or absence of my faith. And that's not to say that when I am grounded in faith, I am not faced with challenging times. It's just that **with faith**, I have found it **easier** to face those challenges.

It was only after embarking on my journey to getting **UNSTUCK** that I began to work on having a relationship with God. I'd like to share some of my experience with you in the hope that I might relieve some of you who might also be feeling challenged in this area.

I grew up in a Catholic family and went to Catholic Church. I attended an all-girls, private Catholic high school. To make a long story short, I did not have a good experience with any of it. When I left home and could make my own decisions, I did not return to church. I believed that God could listen to me anywhere and that I didn't need to step into a building to be heard.

As I matured and began to look back, I realized that my opinions were formed as a teenager. I decided that now that I was an adult and could make more mature decisions, I owed it to myself and to God to return to church and give it a chance.

God led me to a church that felt right for me. The members of that church began to feel like family. And as I continued to attend each week and worship, I would pray for a closeness with him of which I had heard others speak yet had not personally felt before. When I learned to just slow down and connect with my *source* (more on that in Step 5, "Unleash Your Passion"), my conversations with God stopped being one-sided (where *I* did all the talking), and I started to hear *his* message.

Many people who have not yet felt a close relationship with God often want to know what it sounds like when he speaks. It was a question I myself had always wondered. Let me try to explain based on what I have learned from my own experience.

I did not hear a big thundering voice from the clouds. It was more like a thought inside my head, which I just knew God had placed there. There was a sense of peace and absolute knowing in regard to the direction I was being led. He began to guide my steps in a way that I had never felt before. He even helped to write this book. Remember the cocktail party I spoke of at the beginning of this book? I mentioned I had heard a little voice inside my head guiding me with what to do and what props to bring. In hindsight, I now know that little voice was God whispering, "Follow me. I've got your back."

> *"In his heart a man plans his course,*
> *but the Lord determines his steps."*
> —Proverbs 16:9

Picture Yourself Living in B.L.I.S.S.

> *"The secret of achievement is to hold a*
> *picture of a successful outcome in mind."*
> —Henry David Thoreau

So faith is at the center of our **Bliss Points Map**, and I'd now like to invite you to create your own **BPM**. This can be a fun and rewarding activity where you will more easily imagine yourself living in **B.L.I.S.S.** Before we begin, it's important that you understand that our mind thinks in pictures and not in words. By using pictures to create our **BPM**, it serves as a reminder to us of what is important in our lives. And because the main job of our subconscious mind is to complete things or *finish the job*, so to speak, our **BPM** becomes an instruction manual for the subconscious mind to bring those ideals into our reality.

My **BPM** hangs in my office next to my computer. I filled each of the four hearts with words, phrases, quotes, and so on, as well as pictures from magazines, pictures from my computer, and pictures taken from my life, until all the hearts were completely covered with visuals.

The **Bliss Points Map** is similar to a Vision Board in that it contains visuals of what you'd like to manifest in your life. However, unlike a Vision Board, the **BPM** also contains visuals of the elements of your life that you're currently enjoying and would like to continue to nurture. It is created with four hearts and a cross to remind us how to stay healthy on our journey in life. This map combines having gratitude for the things in your present life, along with the vision of your perfect future.

In the health and leisure heart, you'll want to paste visuals that represent being healthy. For example, my health and leisure heart has pictures of me running; a photoshopped picture of me with my ideal, lean body; a heart with a stethoscope to remind me to have regular checkups; healthy foods in lots of different colors; and so on. You'll also want to paste visuals into this heart that represent play and rest, which are just as vital to a healthy lifestyle as exercise and nutrition. I pasted pictures of a baby dancing, a picture of me relaxing poolside while reading a book, pictures of the spa, and so on. ***What do you love to do to relax and unwind?*** Be sure to add that picture to the health and leisure heart on your **BPM**.

For the money and career heart, paste visuals of things you aspire to create in that aspect of your life. In this heart, I pasted the words "Publish a best-selling book," along with a picture of what I thought the cover of this book might look like (before it had been written). I also have a picture of a globe with the words "Financial freedom for all" on my map. Looking at your money and career heart, those visuals are meant to ignite a spark in you. You want them to inspire you to continue to take action steps that will lead to the perfect and ideal situation for you in your career and finances.

The relationships heart is a reminder of those who are important in your life. You'll want it to contain pictures of your spouse or partner, immediate family, children, in-laws, friends, pets, and so on. This heart will also serve as a reminder of the things you aspire to manifest *for* your loved ones. For example, in this heart, I pasted the words "Take my mom on the vacation of her dreams." So on your **BPM**, be sure to add visuals that represent any goals you want to turn into reality for someone that you love.

And finally, in the leaving a legacy heart, you'll want to paste pictures of ways that you want to leave your mark and have a positive impact. The visuals in this heart will represent how you dream of contributing to your community and the world. Let this **B.L.I.S.S.** point be a reminder to you that you are on this earth for a greater purpose. We were all created with very specific DNA that is unique to us. By God's own design, no other human on this planet contains the very same DNA as you. God made you to bring something to this world that ONLY YOU can bring. ***You were born fabulous! And it's time now to share your beautiful gifts with the world.***

Turn on Your Possibility Thinking

> *"If you can dream it, you can do it."*
> —Walt Disney

As you're creating your **BPM**, open your mind and allow yourself to dream really big. Dreaming came to us naturally as kids. If you ever ask a group of children what they want to be when they grow up, many respond not with "I *want* to be . . ." but rather with a very determined and unequivocal "***I am going to be*** . . . an astronaut, a movie star, a spaceship engineer, Miss America, the president of the United States, a race-car driver, a famous ballerina, a veterinarian, and so on." They don't *wish, hope, or want . . . **they declare**.* They don't judge their dreams as being too big, or too small, or even unattainable. They just speak their desired outcome as if it is to be without question. Declare your dreams into reality!

Remember that your **Bliss Points Map** is like the fuel that will help you travel along your path; the next part of navigating your course is to decide on your destination and *write it down*. Where is it that you want to go? If absolutely anything were possible for your life, what comes to mind? What do you envision for your future? How would it feel to live in perfect harmony?

Over the years, as we grow into adulthood, we adopt certain beliefs. Many of them were learned from others (our peers, parents, teachers, society, etc.). The thing to realize is that those beliefs aren't always true nor do they always serve our best and highest self. It is only those supportive beliefs that increase our light and make all our dreams possible. We're going to address this in Step 4, "Train Your Thoughts." For now, let's just agree to start using possibility thinking once again, just as we did as a kid. And remember, "Minds are like parachutes—they work best when open."[5]

Once you're ready to use your *possibility thinking*, it's time to brainstorm so that you can figure out your desired destination on this journey. In this exercise, you're going to want to **WRITE** out your answers. Why is it that writing your answers is so important? Well with all the advances in technology, it seems as though writing is becoming a lost art. Yet it is such a useful tool in exercising our brain for optimal performance. According to a 2010 article from *The Week*, "Study after study suggests that handwriting is important for brain development and cognition."[6] In a 2010 article in the *Wall Street Journal*, Gwendolyn Bounds shares that "some physicians say handwriting could be a good cognitive exercise for baby boomers working to keep their minds sharp as they age."[7] Want to stay sharp? Write out your answers to the following questions.[8]

1. ***What feelings make you come alive?***
   The time I remember that made me feel most alive was the time I _____
   _____.
   When I'm alive, I feel _____
   _____.

2. What would you do ***even if no one paid you to do it?***
   I would _____
   _____
   _____.

3. What would you do ***if you were GUARANTEED to be successful at it?*** If you were ***absolutely CERTAIN*** that it was going to bring you great rewards (monetarily, emotionally, mentally, physically, etc.)?
   I would _____
   _____ and _____ and
   _____.

Write down the first thing that pops into your mind with those questions. And when you're writing, remember to be *in kid mode*. Be free with your imagination and just write down whatever comes to mind—anything and everything. If you feel the need to pause, just sit in silence. Pay attention to your thoughts when you do and then write those down too.

> *"You have powers you never dreamed of. You can do things you never thought you could do. There are no limitations in what you can do except the limitations of your own mind."*
> —Darwin P. Kingsley, 20th-century American leader

For me, the answers that came from those questions were that I wanted ***to inspire others to step into their B.L.I.S.S.***, and the means that I would use to accomplish this were through writing and speaking, both of which *make me come alive*.

Inspire means "to breathe life into."[9] I wanted "to breathe life into" those who felt stuck because I knew what that felt like. I wanted to be able to show them how to bring peace, hope, and joy back into their lives. In order to do so, I first had to find the path to these rewards myself. I had to walk my talk and do all of the steps in this book. I had to muster up my courage, overcome obstacles, step WAY outside of my comfort zone, and persevere when all I wanted to do was retreat. I knew that if I didn't find a way, I would not be able to lead others into **B.L.I.S.S.** either. This turned out to be such a blessing! If it had only been about me, I might have given up. I felt a divine pull to press on no matter what. I had a strong sense that many others were depending on me.

Just like I did, *you* can also muster up your courage; *you* have the strength to persevere. *You*, too, can step outside of your comfort zone and discover some great stepping-stones that will lead you to your highest peak. You were born with amazing abilities, and they are ready and excited for you to tap into them now.

> *"Your vision will become clear only when you can look into your own heart. Who looks outside, dreams. Who looks inside, awakens."*
> —Carl Jung

Completing the exercise of writing down whatever comes to mind with those three questions will help you get back on course. By doing so, you are getting the gears of your imagination lubed up again, and you'll begin to notice more of what's possible in your life. I invite you to keep a journal and begin each day by reviewing these questions and writing what comes to mind.

Expect Detours

> *"If you can find a path with no obstacles,*
> *it probably doesn't lead anywhere."*
> —Unknown

Because your path DOES lead somewhere, you will most likely encounter obstacles along the way. The most important thing is that you continue to find a way to push onward. Remember that it's a detour, not a stop sign. Look for a way over, around, under, or through them to get to where you want to go.

> *"When obstacles arise, you change your direction to reach*
> *your goal; you do not change your decision to get there."*
> —Zig Ziglar

At times, a detour might be what country singer Garth Brooks calls "unanswered prayers." You might have had a certain plan for your life and set out to make it happen. God, on the other hand, might have a bigger and better plan for you than what you had mapped out for yourself. He might have thrown you a detour in order to reroute you onto a greater course that will enable you to discover even more abundant treasures than you ever imagined.

(As a side note, when praying for something, I have learned to ask for "_____ ***or something better***." This shows God that **we** know **HE** knows what's best for us. And although OUR plan is to get _____, his plan might be for something greater in our lives, and this shows that we are open to receiving that.)

I recently had the pleasure of attending a church service where Nick Vujicic was speaking. Nick is "an Australian Christian evangelist and motivational speaker born with tetra-amelia syndrome, a rare disorder characterized by the absence of all four limbs."[10]

Nick shared with us that he had always prayed that God would give him arms and legs. In his prayers, Nick promised that if God did this, he would make it his mission to spread God's will all around the world. He teasingly points out that, to this day, he remains without limbs. Talk about unanswered prayers!

Nick went on to articulate his belief that God had a much bigger plan for him, one that didn't require limbs. Nick was funny, entertaining, joyful, and impactful in his storytelling of the miracles he has been witness to throughout his journey. He paced the stage and sometimes jumped up and down with excitement as he declared God's glory. He told us how he sees himself as more abled than many who were blessed with both arms and legs. Nick said he discovered his passion, his purpose, and his **B.L.I.S.S.** when he stopped trying to plan his own life and began living the life that he believed God had planned for him.

In my life, the first truly big detour that I remember encountering was during my quest to fulfill my dream of becoming a mom—something I had wanted since I was a little girl. My mom and dad had six kids, and I was the second oldest child and the oldest girl. I loved taking care of my younger brothers and sisters, and I've changed a lot of diapers in my lifetime. Growing up, I was called "the little mommy" by my relatives because I took such great care of my younger siblings. Ever since I can remember, I just knew I would grow up to be a mom, and I was very proud of my nurturing abilities and motherly instincts.

The ***detour*** came early on in my marriage when my husband and I discovered that we were infertile and that, without the assistance of modern medicine, we most likely would never know what it would be like to be able to give birth to our baby.

To make a long story short, after many treatments, thousands of dollars out of pocket, and one success that heartbreakingly didn't come to fruition, we decided to put that dream on hold for a while. We both needed a break.

As the years passed and I joined a home-party planning company, I discovered I had a gift for empowering others to reach higher, to achieve more, and to step into their own **B.L.I.S.S.** I built a multimillion-dollar team and was so proud of the women as I watched them transition from anxious and hesitant new business owners into strong, successful, and confident entrepreneurs. In a strange twist of events that I could not have foreseen, I began to fulfill my desire to be a mom. My team became like family to me, and I am so grateful to this day for the blessings God gave me in the friendships that were born from that business.

Looking back on my journey, I had thought that God's plan for me as I reached adulthood was to ***raise children***. I now believe God's plan for me all along has been *to help him **raise people***. It is my sincere hope that, as you get back on course toward living in your own **B.L.I.S.S.**, you, too, will share your journey and empower others so that together we can help to ***raise the world***.

> "Never believe that a few caring people can't change the world. For, indeed, that's all who ever have."
> —Margaret Mead

STEP 3

Start Making Yourself More Visible

"You are the carpenter of your mind. Where you have built a wall, you also have the tools to build a door."
—Valerie Brunnberg

Show Up

There is a tendency when one is in the stuck mode to not want to be seen. Feelings may surface of wanting to sort of hide or blend in or to remain quiet and uninvolved in any conversations. What I've come to realize is that our minds can build walls of protection. Those walls may work for a while, but it is in this stage of our life—when we are ready to get **UNSTUCK** and we've decided to get back on course to living in **B.L.I.S.S.**—that we now want to build a door.

Now is the time to **show up** in your own life. The best way to get **UNSTUCK** is to get around people that are MOVING! Go to leadership conferences, health retreats, and places where people are aspiring to reach new heights in their personal and professional lives. For me, that was one of the greatest perks of running half marathons. I was around thousands of MOVING and motivated people.

I also began going to networking events and small business seminars. At these events, I had to step outside of my comfort zone as I began mingling again, introducing myself to strangers, and allowing myself to feel vulnerable without retreating to the ladies' room.

Once I was attending these events, I got the opportunity to level up by joining a mastermind team. I believe it was Tony Robbins who said, *"If you always do what you've always done, you'll always get what you've always gotten."* If I wanted something different, it was time to **DO** something different. So I made the investment in my future and myself and joined a mastermind team.

A mastermind team is like a big think tank where participants brainstorm together, offering feedback and ideas to help each other excel. It has been my experience that people in mastermind teams have shown a commitment to reaching their potential by investing in themselves and their continuing education. These are the kinds of people you want to be around.

> *"Deliberately seek the company of people who influence you to think and act on building the life you desire."*
> —Napoleon Hill, author of *Think and Grow Rich*

Speak Up

"It takes a lot of courage to show your dreams to someone else."
—Erma Bombeck

In order to *start making yourself more visible*, in addition to **Showing Up**, you'll also want to begin to **Speak Up**. Allow yourself, once again, the opportunity to feel vulnerable and begin engaging in the conversations. Share your thoughts and ideas and contribute to the group. There is a chance that you might feel uncomfortable at first, and that's OK—*allow that*. The only way to get comfortable with what's uncomfortable is through repetition. Continue doing the uncomfortable, and before you know it, *you'll be comfortable with it!*

Remember that your **Bliss Points Map** contains all the reasons that you're on this journey to begin with. Your B.L.I.S.S. points will help you allow this vulnerability and enable you to push forward.

As part of **Speaking Up**, begin sharing the dreams that are in your heart. Start telling others what it is that you'd like to accomplish. Make sure, though, that you are sharing with *like-minded* people. Once again, the mastermind team is one of the very best places to share your ideas, goals, and dreams.

As much as we would like to believe that our loved ones (our spouse, parents, friends, etc.) would be encouraging and always cheering us on toward our goals and dreams, this is not always the case. Sometimes those who love us most might be the ones who discourage us from pursuing a goal and invite us to just play it safe. At times, they might urge us to stay in our comfort zone and to keep from *rocking the boat*.

Why would our loved ones not *always encourage us* to go after our dreams? I believe that, most often, their intentions are good. Sometimes they only want us to experience the good feelings. They may think that by not supporting us, they are somehow helping us reduce any risk. They may also, on some level, sense that *they* may have to change to keep up with us. Therefore, they might want to keep us stagnant so that *they* remain comfortable.

> *"Don't let the noise of others' opinions drown out your own inner voice. And most important, have the courage to follow your heart and intuition. They somehow already know what you truly want to become. Everything else is secondary."*
> —Steve Jobs

If you're a strong-willed person, it might not make a difference to you if you have someone you care about tell you that your idea won't work. But for many, this can cause hesitation and doubt and possibly keep something spectacular from being born. This is precisely why it is so helpful to join a mastermind team or start one yourself. Like-minded people are more likely to encourage you to go for it and to give you ideas on how to get to where it is that you want to go. For me, joining a mastermind group was one of the greatest ways I began to **Show Up** in my own life and regain the confidence to also **Speak Up** and get back on course to living in **B.L.I.S.S**.

Step Up

> *"Everything you need is already within you. The beauty of life is that your DESTINY lies always in your hands. The time has come for you to STEP UP and BE GREAT."*
> —Pablo Valle

You **Step Up** by showing up and speaking up and also by letting go of excuses. You **Step Up** when you begin to have a committed focus on how you show up. Start now to notice when an excuse enters your thoughts and, like the gatekeeper to your dreams, refuse its entry. And then press onward toward the direction of your goals. If that little voice begins to declare, "I can't," change it to the question, "How can I?" Instead of assuming that it's not possible, ask yourself, "If I pretend it might be possible, what are some ways I could make it happen?"

If *lack of time* ever enters your thoughts, remind yourself that we all have the same 24 hours in a day. As Napoleon Hill teaches us, *"Whatever the mind can conceive and believe, it can achieve."*[11] YOU CAN FIND THE TIME to make the necessary changes that will lead you back on the right path. It's a matter of FOCUS.

The best way to focus on finding the time to perform the activities that will produce the results you desire is to keep a written log. I have discovered that when I keep a **mental** to-do list, I spend more time **thinking** about what is on that list (what I have done and what I still need to do). In hindsight, I see that I spent more time **thinking** about my work than I did **working** on my work. I have also discovered that when I get my to-do list out of my head and onto paper, I can accomplish the necessary tasks in one-third of the time.

In addition, when you add a fun element to something that needs to be done, you help engage the brain in actually wanting to do the task. Rather than making to-do lists, I created a **Victory Calendar** for myself. On each day of the week, I would write the word *VICTORY*. Then I'd cover that word with a small sticky note, one for each day. On each sticky note, I would write the most important task that I needed to accomplish for that day—one that would move me closer to my goals. And that is the task I was excited to complete because I got to remove the sticky note and reveal the *VICTORY* underneath. If I didn't do the task, the sticky note had to stay. My brain wanted to see nothing but *VICTORY* all over my calendar.

This also works because, in writing out your sticky note for the next day or even for the week, you have given your subconscious mind a written and focused plan. It will now work to bring you the resources necessary to accomplish that task.

Be sure that the task you are writing on your sticky note has been chunked down into baby steps too. You'll be more likely to complete it that way. Instead of writing "Finish my book" on a note (that would be a daunting task for one day), I might write "Spend one focused hour writing my book." Instead of "Clean out the garage," I might write "Fill one box with items from the garage that I am donating to charity."

By working with a **Victory Calendar** in this manner, you will be amazed at how much more you will begin to accomplish with the time that you have.

As you're working toward your goals, another thought that might come into your head is *lack of money*. If you have this thought, I invite you to think of that as a wall that you have built up in your mind and remember that you have the ability to now build a door that can lead you to great wealth. Remember that "success comes in CANS, not cannots!"[12] Stepping up means finding a way over, under, through, or around. I'll give you an example.

When business conferences were being announced in my community, I contacted the facilitator and offered my assistance, which she gratefully accepted. I arrived early, looked around and analyzed where I thought I could be of service, and got to work doing whatever I could to help things run smoothly for the event. Sometimes that was merely helping out at the registration table. Other times, I'd be a "gofer," where I would just run here and there, doing and getting whatever the event organizer needed. I am mainly talking about being of service to others. I wanted to do such an excellent job for her that she would feel as though she couldn't have an event without me!

Because of this, many three-day conferences, which would have cost me thousands of dollars in order to participate, I attended for free.

Many event organizers will waive your registration fee if you influence a certain number of people to register for the event. In this case, your influence becomes like "cash in the bank." Change statements such as "I can't afford to attend" to a question that can lead to open possibilities such as *"How can I be of service in this situation?"*

It's important to note that not once have I *asked* for a free ticket, nor would I ever *expect* one. Rather, I searched for a way to be of great service **without any expectations**. As Zig Ziglar has often stated, "You can have everything in life you want if you'll just help enough other people get what they want."[13]

Another great question to ask yourself might be *"What would I need to do to be able to make this investment?"* If your job allows you to pick up extra hours to bring in additional income, that could be one option for you. Perhaps you could organize a garage sale to raise the necessary funds. Maybe there is a gift-giving occasion approaching such as your birthday or Christmas, and you know someone that typically enjoys giving you a present. You could let your loved ones know that the registration would make the perfect gift, and they would be investing in your future. The phenomenal growth of the Internet has made group altruism possible; you may want to consider crowdfunding to raise money for your project.

Stepping up means finding a way! It means being willing to play a bigger game. Better yet, it means, getting **IN** the game! You can't play by sitting on the sidelines. As the saying goes, "Life is not a spectator sport."[14] You've got to get out onto that field, jump into the arena, sprint to that track, and be ready to play full out! When you begin to **Show Up**, **Speak Up**, and **Step Up** once again, making yourself visible to the world, you will be the game changer your dreams need to get you back on course to living in **B.L.I.S.S**.

STEP 4

Train Your Thoughts

*"**Watch your thoughts**, for they become words. Choose your words, for they become actions. Understand your actions, for they become habits. Study your habits, for they become your character. Develop your character, for **it becomes your destiny**."*
—Unknown

Watch What You're Thinking:
Words, Actions, Thoughts, Character, Habits

Train your thoughts? Yes! You can train the way you think so that you're producing greater results in your life. The old adage is true: "What we think about is what we bring about." The first step to training our thoughts is to begin to **pay closer attention to what it is we're actually thinking**. If our thoughts eventually lead us to our destiny, then by changing our thoughts, we can change our destiny, too—hence the saying, "***The best way to predict your future is to create it.***"[15]

Did you know that the average person has about 70,000 thoughts per day and that the majority of those thoughts are negative?[16] Most of the time we aren't consciously aware of what we're thinking and how it is affecting our choices and our physiology. Here is the wonderful thing. Once you start ***paying attention*** to your thoughts and you understand how to analyze what is serving you for your greater good and what is not, you can become an advocate for better thinking in your own mind and better results in your physical world as well.

I'm referring to psychoneuroimmunology, the study of the mind/body connection. *Merriam-Webster's Dictionary* defines it as "a field of medicine that deals with the influence of emotional states (as stress) and nervous system activity on immune function especially in relation to their effect on the onset and progression of disease."[17] Research shows that our thoughts can have a direct impact on the way we feel. Negative thoughts actually release chemicals in our bodies that weaken our physiology and lower our immune system. In his book *Ageless Body, Timeless Mind*, author and physician Deepak Chopra states, "Our cells are constantly eavesdropping on our thoughts and being changed by them."[18] He goes on to say, "Wherever thought goes, a chemical goes with it."[19] These thoughts can put our body at *dis*-ease and, over time, without being addressed, can bring *disease*. Conversely, positive thoughts release chemicals in our bodies that strengthen our physiology and boost our immune system.

The key to making the change that can bring us greater health is to take those negative thoughts off of autopilot and begin to consciously take back control of your thinking. When people have been in stuck mode for a while, there is often a little voice instructing them *not to rock the boat*. There are different names for that voice, such as monkey chatter or ego. That little voice is your mind attempting to communicate with you, and as it gets more insistent, its power may increase. Think of it like an old program running on the *internal hard-drive* of your mind. This old program keeps repeating that which you've made a habit until you learn to *upload* a newer and more efficient program. Imagine it as though you need to install a new version of Windows so that your computer gets up to speed. Even if you make a change that can take you forward into joy, with that old program running in the background, it can hamper your efforts. The good news is **YOU *have the power to override that little voice!*** It's time for YOU to upload a new program and get back on course to your abundantly blessed future.

Choose Your Words

Although I have always done my best to look on the bright side and worked to be a positive thinker, it wasn't until I studied with Dr. Yvonne Oswald that I learned the magnitude to which our thoughts control the outcomes in our lives. In her book *Every Word has Power*, Dr. Yvonne Oswald teaches how to "switch on your language and turn on your life." She says, "By consciously switching your words and directing your thoughts, you transform not only your perception of life but also your results."[20]

The reason our thoughts and words are so important to what we bring about in our reality is because of what our subconscious mind does with them. Let me explain. Our subconscious mind is like a great big computer, and its primary jobs are to keep us alive and also to complete things or to *finish the job* that it *thinks* we gave it. It's important to know that our subconscious mind does not hear negatives, and, like an Internet search, it only focuses on keywords. So, if I say to you, "Do not think about a bright red sports car right now," what happens? Your mind immediately pictures a bright red sports car. If you did an Internet search and typed into the search engine the words "do not think about a bright red sports car," what would the search engine pull up? It accesses pictures and articles about a bright red sports car, right? That is how our subconscious mind works too.

If you say, "Don't worry," you're actually telling your subconscious mind to worry. If you say, "No problem," you're actually telling your subconscious mind that there is a problem. Those are what Dr. Yvonne Oswald labels as "low-energy"[21] words and phrases, and they can, as I mentioned earlier, weaken the immune system and bring more problems and worry.

To "switch" your words, Dr. Yvonne Oswald suggests that sometimes it works best to think in opposites. For example, if it's "not a problem," what is it? "It's my pleasure!" This phrase uses "high-energy"[22] words to say what you were intending to say and will bring about more positive results than the former. What is the opposite of *worry*? Maybe it is "faith"? So then "Don't worry" becomes "Have faith" or "You'll be fine." By changing your low-energy words to high-energy words, you're sending your subconscious mind out to bring you *pleasure and faith* versus asking it to bring you *problems and worry*. (For more examples of low-energy and high-energy words, see the table in the appendix.)

As you practice watching your thoughts, you'll begin to identify those low-energy words, and you'll learn to choose the higher-energy ones that will bring greater results in your life. Dr. Yvonne Oswald suggests getting a "switch buddy"[23] who can point out when you've just said low-energy words. All they have to say when they hear you using them is "Switch!", at which point your job is to rephrase what you said with a higher-energy word or phrase. It's a matter of becoming more aware and then making a simple change. This simple practice will have profound results in your life.

Change Your Story

"It's not who you are that holds you back; it's who you think you're not."
—Unknown

Often, when in the stuck mode, feelings of inferiority can surface. The monkey chatter can send us all kinds of thoughts attempting to lead us to believe that we might never be as good as "xyz."

The first time I was around my mastermind group, I noticed as everyone introduced themselves that I was among very accomplished authors, radio talk show hosts, singers, actresses, very successful CEO's, and so on. My monkey chatter was telling me that these people were far more qualified to belong to this group than I was. *"Look at them, and look at you,"* it said. *"You haven't written a book. You don't have a radio show. You don't even have a bachelor's degree. What do YOU know? You don't belong in this <u>room</u>, much less in this <u>group</u>. When they find out how unqualified you are, you'll be kicked out of the group for sure!"* If we had a friend that said such negative comments to us all the time, we'd surely end that relationship, right?

"The bad things are easier to believe."
—Julia Roberts's character in *Pretty Woman*

One reason we might believe the "bad things" can be because of something we might have learned as a child. Let me give you an example. I grew up in a family that loved to tease, pull pranks, poke fun, and so on. With five siblings, a common phrase among us was *"You're so stupid."* If one of us answered a question incorrectly, we were laughed at and teased relentlessly.

Isn't it ironic (or *is* it?) that one of the fears I carried into adulthood was for someone to consider me *stupid*? I would often go to great lengths to avoid this feeling, sometimes *pretending to know* something I didn't because I believed I was *supposed* to know it. Notice how by pretending to know something we don't, we turn away (by not asking for clarification) new knowledge and, in effect, bring on more of the keyword *stupid* we sent to the subconscious mind and asked it to bring us.

Based on Dr. Yvonne Oswald's "Switch" concept mentioned earlier, I now understand the importance of replacing that low-energy word with the phrase "not smart." I am still professing the same emotion, yet in a more positive serving manner. This simple change directs the subconscious mind to bring me the resources that will actually make me smarter!

Even though I was very accomplished as an adult, that old program was still operating and it triggered that "Not smart" feeling as I was attempting to get **UNSTUCK**. When I was stepping outside my comfort zone and doing new things like joining a mastermind team, that little voice was like a loved one that didn't want me to get hurt. It didn't want me to have that feeling, so it said, *"Stay here where you're safe. No one will call you stupid here. Everything is good right where you are."* But I could no longer stay where I was. I'd had enough. It was time to take a risk. Now that I knew about the impact my thoughts and words could have on my future, it was time to change some of the stories I had been telling myself for far too long. It was time to live "Happily ever after."

> *"And the day came when the risk to remain tight in a bud was more painful than the risk it took to blossom."*
> —Anaïs Nin

Thankfully, once you understand about limiting beliefs and how to correct them and once you begin *watching your thoughts* and *choosing your words*, you can then *change your story* to one that will lead you to a much happier destination.

You'll notice that in the first four chapters of this book, there are some low-energy words and phrases. I kept them in because they were important to the story. I wanted you to understand that ***I know how you feel. I have felt that same way myself.*** And what I have found is that ***there is a way to get back on top of the world again.***

So far, we have discussed **Using Today** to make the decision to get UNSTUCK, to begin taking those baby steps, and to prepare to climb back up that mountain. We've talked about how to **Navigate Your Course** by getting clear on your *WHY* and using your **B.L.I.S.S. Points Map**. We've mentioned that you'll want to turn on your possibility thinking and to also expect detours along the way, knowing that it is OK. We've encouraged you to **Start Making Yourself More Visible** by showing up, speaking up, and stepping up. And we've shared how to **Train Your Thoughts** by first watching them and then making better word choices so that ultimately you can change your story and create a better outcome!

It's Now Time to Step into Your **B.L.I.S.S.**
*B*ecause *L*ife *Is* *S*o *S*pectacular

STEP 5

Unleash Your Passion

*"The two most important days in your life are the day
you were born, and the day you find out why."*
—Mark Twain

Ask Questions to Spark Your Passion

Merriam-Webster's Dictionary defines *passion* as "a strong feeling of enthusiasm or excitement for something or about doing something."[24] It is that strong feeling of enthusiasm that fuels our persistence and determination and allows us the ability to press on no matter what. When you find your passion, it is as though you've discovered why you were born.

As we move to step outside our comfort zone and create new patterns in our life, our passion enables us to continue onward. One of the best ways to activate our passion is to review our **Bliss**

Points Map. This will remind us of all the amazing treasures that are currently in our lives, as well as the ones we are working to achieve.

The saying "Where there is a will there is a way" refers to this very passion. Passion enables the mind to *find* a way. Passion opens up the mind to the possibilities and allows us to see new ways of making something happen. Passion doesn't think about the reasons a goal can't be accomplished. It only asks the question "How can I?" and then finds resources to come up with the solutions to show us how to reach the desired outcome.

When I decided that I wanted to write this book, my monkey chatter was quick to remind me that I was not an author. It pointed out that I didn't know the first thing about writing a book, and it kept playing that old program in my head.

And it was Passion that said, *"Let's do this! Sounds exciting. I can find a way. If I WERE to write a book, what would that look like? What would it sound like to be called an 'author'? What would it feel like? What would I need to do to get started? Who could I talk to for guidance? When could I begin? Where could I go to find the inspiration to fuel the writing? Why would writing this book be important to me and to others?"*

Passion asks the questions that continue to fuel the passion. It's like a self-charging battery. If negative statements come up, make the decision to change those thoughts to questions. Unleash your passion by asking yourself the "Who?," "What?," "When?," "Where?," and "Why?" questions that can assist you in getting to your desired destination.

> *Whom can I talk to for guidance?*
> *What would I need to do to get started?*
> *What would ONE BABY STEP be toward this goal?*

When might I begin?
Where could I go for inspiration?
Why would accomplishing this be important to me?

These questions, along with your **Bliss Points Map**, will help you develop what Zig Ziglar calls your "yearning power."

*"You enhance your chances for success when you understand that your **yearning** power is more important than your **earning** power."*
—Zig Ziglar

Plug Yourself in and Get Reenergized

"We are actually taking better care of our smartphones than we are of ourselves."
—Arianna Huffington

In addition to asking yourself some thought-provoking questions that can unleash your passion, it is also important to ***plug yourself in*** and get reenergized! When was the last time you *disconnected* from technology and *connected* to your source? Many of us live in a fast-paced world and perceive the pace of the world around us as one that is necessary for us to adopt as our own. I have learned that it is in the *slowing down* that we can actually get to our destination faster.

I have met so many people who are longing for more peace and harmony in their lives, and often it's really simple to acquire it. For many people, it would just take having a focused awareness on slowing down. When we unplug from our smartphones, televisions, computers, laptops, and mobile devices, we are, in essence, quieting the noise of the outside world so that we can allow the voice of our inside world—or our spirit—to be heard.

Let's be clear here. I am not suggesting a world of no technology. I am merely suggesting that you spend **some** focused time each day, where you unplug from it and plug into your spirit. Dedicate some quiet time just for you. One of the very best times to do this is first thing in the morning, even if it means setting your alarm to go off 10 minutes earlier than normal. I recommend making a date with your spirit for when you arise each day. You will be amazed at how much better time flows for you when you do this.

> *"Quietness is the classroom where*
> *you learn to hear my voice."*
> —Sarah Young, *Jesus Calling*, passage for October 30

Find a quiet spot where you can be alone in the stillness. It might even be just staying in bed and beginning to have a focused awareness on your breathing. My favorite morning quiet spot is outside in my swing and with my coffee. I find that it's best to begin with gratitude. Simply say thanks for the blessings that are in your life and then set your intentions for that day. Remember that we get what we focus on. You are the designer of your days. Your life is a result of all the choices that you've made or not made throughout the years. When you begin each morning with the act of setting an intention for that day, you will produce the difference between making things happen versus just letting things happen.

You might ask yourself these questions:

How will I choose to live this very day?
If today were my perfect day, what would that look/sound/feel like?

Who would I spend time with?
What activities would I be doing?
What is one thing I can do today that will bring me **B.L.I.S.S.***?*

And if today is a workday for you, you might ask the following:

What could I do to make my workday a perfect day?
How will I make it pleasurable?
When I lay my head down on my pillow tonight, what is it that I will have done that will give me a wonderful sense of peace, joy, and accomplishment?

By taking some time first thing in the morning to be grateful for the abundance that is in your life, you're giving your subconscious mind direction to bring you more. And by setting the intention for your day, you're directing your subconscious mind to also bring you the resources you're going to need in order to bring those intentions to reality.

In addition to taking some time for you, you'll also want to dedicate some quiet time each day for those you love. Let me ask you something. Have you noticed how prevalent smartphones are in restaurants these days? When we release our need to engage with those who aren't in our presence and begin to spend time **truly being present** with those who are, we improve our relationships, we achieve a greater sense of harmony, and we become more conscious of the blessings that surround us.

My girlfriends and I recently started a rule that we wouldn't touch our smartphones when we were dining together—with the only exception being to take some fun pictures. It was more challenging than we anticipated, as we didn't realize how much we were used to reaching for them. We had a habit of checking an email, looking at our texts/tweets/posts, and so on. We soon began to discover that our conversations were so much more engaging and full of life when we left our phones in our purses. We were, in a sense, plugging into each other. We could feel a greater sense of connection than we had previously known during those times when we were more apt to be on our phones.

I remember the days before we had smartphones. We would get in our car to go someplace, and there would be absolutely no distractions except for the world going on immediately outside our car—other cars, billboards, buildings, and so on. We actually noticed the homes and businesses that we were driving past. We did not need sign spinners dancing on the side of the street to try to get our attention. We were very much aware of our surroundings. We were connected. And we could just listen to music and be at peace getting from one place to the next.

Guess what? That hasn't changed. We still can do all these things. It is a choice. You can choose to plug into technology, or you can choose to plug into your spirit. It is the latter that will bring you the energy to get you to where you want to go.

Sharpen Your Senses to Increase Your Blessings

"Not the senses that I have but what I do with them is my kingdom."
—Helen Keller

By learning to slow down and unplug from technology, we can begin to work on sharpening our senses that might have been dulled by the fast pace at which we have been attempting to live our lives. In doing this, we learn how to become proactive in our lives instead of being reactive to that which wants our energy and might not be worthy of it. We are able to make better choices in our lives that will lead to the sweet success that we desire.

You might be amazed at how calming the act of slowing down can be. It may surprise you to realize your ability to slow down time when you slow down your own thinking and become more focused and aware of the present moment. It takes a little bit of practice, and yet it is a simple activity that you can begin to put into place today.

- Start by just observing your breathing.
- Imagine your stomach is a balloon, and when you take a deep breath in through your nose, you want that oxygen to fill up that balloon.
- As you exhale through your mouth, imagine that the balloon is releasing all that air as your stomach returns to its natural state.
- Each time you inhale and fill up your balloon, imagine inhaling lots of good, healthy, clean, vibrant energy into every cell of your body.
- Each time you exhale through your mouth, imagine letting go of that which is not needed in order to serve your higher purpose.

Practicing this simple breathing technique is like a massage for your spirit and will help you perform your daily routines more efficiently.

In addition to putting this breathing technique into play, it is also a healthy practice to spend some time each day with a focused awareness of your surroundings and how they contribute to your five senses. Living in South Florida, I love to spend time outdoors inhaling the salty air around me. I marvel at the energy that takes place in nature and contemplate how that energy connects us all.

"You are not a drop in the ocean. You are the entire ocean in a drop."
—Rumi

On a typical morning, I practice gazing at my surroundings like a small child filled with wonder and delight. I see the masterpiece of nature that God painted for us—the beautiful hues of green in the trees and the grass. I feel the same breeze brushing my skin that is also making the palm fronds sway gently above me, and I delight in the connectedness of that energy. I watch the soft white billowing clouds slowly drift across the pale blue sky. Off in the distance, I hear the sweet song of a bird faintly singing in the background. Two yellow butterflies are dancing along the hedge, reminding me that life holds many opportunities to have fun and be playful.

I am grateful for the ability to see, hear, smell, taste, and touch, and I whisper my thanks to God for these gifts. I thank God for the opportunities that the day holds and ask him to help me be my very best so that I may, in turn, bring out the best in the lives of those around me. I ask him to bring peace and comfort to those who are not happy, not feeling loved, or not well. I thank God for my **B.L.I.S.S.**, and then I begin my day.

Turn Your Passion into Action

> *"She believed in dreams, all right. But she also believed in doing something about them. When Prince Charming didn't come along, she went over to the palace and got him."*
> —Walt Disney on *Cinderella*

At this point on your journey, you are ready to **turn that passion into ACTION**. Hoping, praying, imagining, thinking, wishing . . . these work when **YOU** get to work! And you'll want to use your **B.L.I.S.S. Points Map** from Step 2, "Navigate Your Course," to begin figuring out your action steps.

Let's review the four hearts that are all grounded in faith and are represented by the cross:

1. Relationships, friends, and family
2. Health and leisure
3. Money and career
4. Leaving a legacy

What actions can you take in each of these areas to bring you closer to your dreams? If a sense of being overwhelmed occurs, remember to break the action down into manageable pieces. You might start by simply asking yourself, "Which of the four hearts needs a little love this week in order to beat stronger?"

Let's use health and leisure as an example. Perhaps you have a little whisper telling you that there is something to which you need to be paying attention. It might be a mammogram or colonoscopy you've been putting off, the dental cleaning that would keep your gums and teeth healthy, a visit to the eye doctor to have your eyesight checked, and so on. Your action step is simply to pick up the phone and make an appointment for the very next time that is available. If it's after hours, add this simple step to a sticky note and place it on tomorrow's date in your **Victory Calendar**.

> *"Take care of your body. It's the only place you have to live."*
> —Jim Rohn

So I'll ask you again: taking a look at your **Bliss Points Map**, which heart needs a little love this week? ***Check off only one for now.***

☐ Relationships, friends, and family
☐ Health and leisure

☐ Money and career
☐ Leaving a legacy

What action step can you take that will help that heart to beat stronger? *Fill in the following blanks:*

*I know that when I _____
_____, _____
_____this
B.L.I.S.S. point will once again beat stronger. When all four B.L.I.S.S. points are beating strong, I have greater health physically, mentally, and spiritually. Because of this, today/tomorrow (depending on whether you do this exercise in the morning when you arise or in the evening before going to bed), I will be/do/have_____
_____
_____.*

Now add this action step to your sticky note and put it in your **Victory Calendar**. I recommend that every night before you go to bed, you do this exercise in preparation for a great day to follow.

When you begin to ask the questions that spark your passion and you learn to slow down, plug into your spirit, and sharpen your senses, you will notice more of the abundant blessings that are all around you. This allows your passion to grow like a plant being nurtured with the proper soil, sun, and water. Then the *action* part is what is going to assist you in turning those dreams into reality.

STEP 6

Celebrate Something Each Day

*"As we let our own light shine, we unconsciously
give others permission to do the same."*
—Marianne Williamson

Celebrate YOU

You were born fabulous! God created each of us with the most amazing gifts and talents, and too often, we don't allow ourselves the full opportunity to shine. By the time we reach adulthood, many of us have adopted a habit of squelching our brilliance. Maybe we learned that celebrating our accomplishments would be considered boastful. Perhaps we falsely believed that other people's gifts would not be recognized unless we denied or at least diminished our own.

But as Marianne Williamson reminds us in the previous quote, it is just the opposite. When we allow ourselves the freedom to bask in the glory of our own internal gifts, others are able to receive the gift of our spirit, and in turn, we give them the freedom to allow their own spirit to shine brighter. How many times have you received a compliment and actually said thank you and allowed your spirit to simply enjoy the praise?

For years, I have bought Oprah Winfrey's magazine O strictly for her "What I Know for Sure" article always found on the last page. It so resonates with me that it often feels as if she was reading my thoughts. My most favorite one was in her February 2003 issue where she talks about how we sometimes deflect praise. In it, Oprah says, "Instead of being filled with all the passion and purpose that enable us to offer our best to the world, we empty ourselves in an effort to silence our critics." When we diminish our light in order to try to silence these critics, they win. Wouldn't life be so much grander if we each allowed our light to shine as bright as God intended, showing others through our example that it is OK to shine?

It's time to start a celebration revolution! Starting today, learn to celebrate your gifts. When someone pays you a compliment, pause and give yourself time to receive it. Breathe it into your spirit and say "thank you," and allow it to fill you up so that your spirit shines even brighter. Starting today, celebrate who you are! Celebrate every cell, organ, and bone in your body. Celebrate your brilliance! Celebrate your beauty! Celebrate your life!

Celebrate by Being Grateful

> *"If the only prayer you said in your whole life was 'thank you,' that would suffice."*
> —Meister Eckhart

As I recommended in Step 5, "Unleash Your Passion," it's best to start each day with gratitude for the blessings in your life. When you begin each day with gratitude, the world often brings you even more treasures. Your gratefulness has the ability to turn each day into a celebration.

Chances are, you have numerous blessings for which to be grateful! There is a saying: "Someone else is happy with less than what you have." Imagine how abundantly blessed you are! There are many individuals who cannot answer yes to the following questions. If you *can* answer *yes*, consider the last time you said, "thank you" for these rich and abundant blessings.

- Can you move your limbs of your own free will?
- Can you read the words in this book?
- Can you see? Hear? Taste? Smell? Feel?
- Do you have a roof over your head?
- Do you have food in your kitchen?
- Do you have clean water to drink?
- Do you have a working toilet, bath, or shower?
- Do you have money in the bank or in your wallet?
- Do you have a place to sleep?
- Do you feel safe and secure?
- Do you have a way to travel to where you need to go?
- Do you breathe on your own without the assistance of any machines?
- Do you know how very blessed you are?
- Do you give thanks for all these things each day?

Imagine if, when you awoke tomorrow, you only had that which you were grateful for today! Each day, I recommend that you begin by giving thanks for all the abundant blessings in your life: blessings that have been freely given to you in all shapes, colors, and sizes. This morning exercise is one of the best ways to celebrate each day.

Celebrate by Activating Your Endorphins

Endorphins are a drug that our bodies naturally produce. They are "biochemical substances made by the body that reduce pain and bring about a feeling of euphoria and well-being."[22] Strenuous exercise (such as heavy weight lifting or a highly aerobic activity like running) has been found to signal the body to release these feel-good chemicals. And, according to an article on WebMD.com, even moderate exercise has the ability to increase your sense of happiness. Biking, dancing, yoga, running, walking, and even gardening can elevate your positive energy.[23]

I know that for me, whenever I make a point of moving my body, whether through running, Zumba, weight training, or just going for a walk, I feel better about myself. I have a greater sense of happiness and calm. It also seems to produce a higher level of focus and clarity for me. So RUN! If you don't like to run, then walk. If you don't like to walk, then bike. If you don't like to bike, then swim. If you don't like to swim, then dance. The point is that it's beneficial to your happiness level and sense of well-being to just get moving! Of course, if it's been a while since you've exercised, you'll want to check with your doctor to find out what level is safe for you to get started. If you need to check with your doctor first, be sure to add a sticky note to your **Victory Calendar** for tomorrow. Write on your note, "Call doc to discuss exercise routine" and then follow through so you can achieve your victory.

Celebrate by Playing

One of the B.L.I.S.S. points on your **BPM** is health and leisure. As I mentioned in Step 2, "Navigate Your Course," play and rest are just as important to a healthy lifestyle as exercise! When was the last time you did something fun? Children naturally play all the time. As adults, sometimes we take ourselves too seriously. When was the last time you allowed yourself to be silly? When was the last time you had a good, deep belly laugh (when you laughed until tears rolled down your face)? Laughter truly is the best medicine, and if you don't take the time for play and rest, you won't find much laughter in your life either.

One of my favorite aspects of running long distances with my girlfriends is when we dress up in costumes and bring smiles to the faces of those around us. Often, we'll wear tutus and tiaras and run along the beach in Fort Lauderdale, Florida, eliciting smiles, honks, and finger pointing. You get the idea. I'll be the first to admit that often I can be too serious, and it's times like this that remind me how healthy it is to let loose and have some fun. Plus, it feels so great to make other people happy. I think in doing this, we are reminding others through our example that it's OK to have some fun. Playtime is not just for kids!

Celebrate by Giving

> *"Whenever you see darkness, there is extraordinary opportunity for the light to burn brighter."*
> —Bono

Ever notice that when you're not feeling happy and you perform an act of kindness for someone else, it always lifts your spirits? I'll never forget the year I went to buy a ham for Christmas. When I arrived at the store, there was a line out the door and around the plaza of people waiting to buy their own holiday ham. I had so much to do that day and wasn't happy about having to wait in that line, but I made the most of it. I even came up with an idea I was so excited about that it made the line seem to move faster. When I finally made it to the counter, I ordered two hams—one for me and one to give away. I decided to go to the very back of the line where the most recent people to join were probably feeling as anxious as I was when I had first arrived. I asked, "Is there anyone here who just needs to buy a ham?" I figured that some were also getting pies and side dishes, and my goal was to save someone from having to wait in that line. I gave my ham to the first woman that said yes and raised her hand. You would have thought I had given her a million dollars. And it made me feel like a million bucks!

Be aware that giving doesn't have to cost money. You can give a hug, a compliment, your time, a smile, and so on. It's also good to be cognizant that there may be times when your giving isn't as well received as you would have liked. Perhaps you smiled at someone who didn't smile back, or maybe your smile was returned by a cross look. I invite you to think of that person as a hybrid car that hasn't connected to its power source in a long time and has, therefore, run out of fuel. Your smile or greeting may give that person just enough energy to get back to his or her source and get plugged in again.

Celebrate the Little Things

I hope that, by now, you're really appreciating the magnitude of everything you have to celebrate. And there are so many things you can do to have a celebration! Here is a list of numerous ways that you can reward yourself and celebrate each day.

Take a bubble bath; light a candle; eat cake and ice cream for no reason; watch the sunset; watch the sunrise; listen to the ocean waves; laugh; put a paper umbrella in your drink; have your hair shampooed by someone who knows how to give a good scalp massage; pet a dog; cuddle with someone you love; listen to songs of praise; sing out loud; look through pictures of loved ones; buy a bouquet of flowers at the store and give them away to a stranger; listen to music that makes your heart sing; dance like no one's watching; get a massage; walk barefoot in the grass; go to the beach; enjoy a frozen beverage on a hot day; enjoy a hot beverage on a cold day; spend some quiet time with God; go for an early morning run; use your best china at dinner for no reason; smell some honeysuckles; watch butterflies; have a heart-to-heart conversation; plant something and watch it grow; make something with your own two hands; tithe; take a hike in nature and admire God's handiwork; collect seashells; cuddle with a kitten; call an old friend out of the blue and tell them how much you love them; chew a piece of gum and see how big of a bubble you can blow; eat popcorn while watching a movie; do a handstand in the swimming pool; do a cannonball in the swimming pool; eat dessert before dinner; take a bike ride; buy new pillows; wear sexy lingerie under your clothes; rock a baby; swing or seesaw with a child; buy new bed sheets and make them smell like an ocean breeze; slide down a slide; play miniature golf; get a pedicure; perform a random act of kindness; share a hug with someone; skip; find pictures in the clouds; send a handwritten card to someone just because; bake something; make someone's favorite recipe and give it to them for no special occasion; laugh; watch a movie that makes you cry; have a tea party; buy some jewelry that makes you feel extra sparkly; put a candle in your dessert and make a wish before you blow it out; wear fuzzy socks or slippers. Fill in the blanks with any others that come to mind.

_____
_____
_____

And finally, make a point to celebrate something TODAY!

> *"The more you praise and celebrate your life,*
> *the more there is in life to celebrate."*
> —Oprah Winfrey

STEP 7

Keep Your Commitments

"Commitment—the man on top of the mountain didn't fall there."
—Anonymous

One of the best things you can do to stay on course is to keep your commitments. When you make a commitment, you have set an intention of something that you are going to see through to the end. Each time you keep your commitment you exercise your consistency muscle and build the healthy practice of completing your intentions. When you don't keep your commitments, you build the practice of not doing the things you said you were going to do and you can quickly find yourself getting off course.

Make a List

> *"When you say yes to others, make sure you are not saying no to yourself."*
> —Paulo Coelho

You've got to make yourself a priority in your life! Often, when people find themselves having to back out of a commitment, it is because they have overextended themselves. Have you ever said yes to others so many times that you have neglected your personal health and well-being? In order to be able to keep your commitments and also stay on course for what's right in your life, I recommend that you begin by setting some rules for yourself that become nonnegotiable. By setting up some personal guidelines, you might find it easier to say no to something or someone when you're being asked to give time that you don't have to give.

Take a look at your **Bliss Points Map**. What might be nonnegotiable in the area of friends and family? Let me give you an example. Maybe as a family, you have committed to spending Sundays together, and this is nonnegotiable. So if someone invites you to an event or asks you to do something on a Sunday, you merely tell them that you have reserved Sundays for your family, and it is one of your nonnegotiable commitments. You could politely let them know you'd be happy to do something with or for them on a Saturday, for example.

What might be nonnegotiable in the area of health and leisure? Perhaps you go to the gym on Tuesday and Thursday mornings. You know that keeping this commitment to yourself keeps you fit mentally, emotionally, and physically. So saying yes to anything that keeps you from going to the gym on these days would not be good for your health. Therefore your Tuesday and Thursday morning workouts are nonnegotiable.

Take some time now to write down some of your nonnegotiable commitments in each of the areas of your **Bliss Points Map**.

1. Health and leisure

    In order to maintain my health and to have some time for play and rest, my nonnegotiable commitment in this area of my life is _____.

2. Relationships, friends, and family

    In order to spend quality time with my friends and family so that I maintain healthy relationships, my nonnegotiable commitment in this area of my life is _____.

3. Money and career

    In order to build a healthy career and financial portfolio, my nonnegotiable commitment in this area of my life is _____.

4. Leaving a legacy

    In order to pursue my passion and my purpose and contribute to the world around me, my nonnegotiable commitment in this area of my life is _____.

    I understand that my four B.L.I.S.S. points are healthiest when they are grounded in my relationship with God. So in order to stay in close communication and to grow my faith, my nonnegotiable commitment in this area of my life is _____.

Once you have created your list and before you commit to anything, review your nonnegotiable commitments. You'll be better equipped to say no to the invitations that do not fit into your healthy life plan.

Keep Your Commitment to God

> *"But seek first the kingdom of God and his righteousness, and all these things will be added to you."*
> —Matthew 6:33

I have shared throughout this book that it's a healthy practice to make some time each day to sit quietly and work on communicating with God. By reserving as little as five minutes each day just to be still, to reflect, and to give gratitude for your blessings, you will transform your life for the better. Remember the cross is the center of your **Bliss Points Map**. It is what keeps the oxygen flowing and the blood pumping. By spending quality time working on connecting with your source, you are breathing life into each of the four hearts on your **Bliss Points Map**. When you practice daily your communication with God, you are allowing your spirit the greatest chance to soar.

Keep Your Commitment to Others

Sometimes we back out of situations that are completely in our control without realizing it or stopping to think about what it might mean to the other person. For example, there are many professions that trade their time for money. When you make an appointment with hairdressers or nail technicians for example, they block that time out for you and promise that it is yours and no one else's. You promise that you will pay them in return for the service provided in that block of time. Their blocked spaces of time are limited, and the payment made for those time slots is how they earn a living. When you cancel an appointment at the last minute and the time slot cannot be filled, you most likely don't know what effect that might have on their life. Nor do you know how many others have also done the same thing. If you were still going to be charged the same fee, regardless of whether or not you kept the appointment, would you show up? Ask yourself that question the next time you're thinking of canceling, and if your answer is yes, then keep your commitment!

I also want you to think about the times when you've made a personal date with someone. When you make plans to get together (for lunch, dinner, a cup of coffee, etc.), you most likely have no idea how much that date might mean to that person. And again, they have set aside that time for you. Honor them and show them respect by keeping that commitment. To illustrate how important this is, let me share a story with you.

My friend and I were out of town for a race, and it happened to be in the town where her elderly aunt lived. This woman had recently survived some serious health challenges. We invited her to join us for dinner the first night we were to arrive. We did not know it at the time, but she was so excited that she went to the salon that day and had her hair and nails done for the occasion. Imagine if we had canceled on her! My heart is heavy at the thought of people backing out on the Aunt Elizabeths of the world that have been sitting at home in excited anticipation. So before canceling on someone, consider what effect that might have on the other person and do your best to keep your commitment.

There have been many times on my journey that I wanted to back out of certain commitments. For example, when I was working on Step 3, "Start Making Yourself More Visible," I began setting some lunch dates to connect with business women in the area to see how we might best support each other's growth. Because this was a new practice for me, it was outside of my comfort zone, and my mental chatter often urged me to cancel that date. I would often have thoughts of not having enough time and having too many other things to do. Without practicing conscious awareness, I would have almost unconsciously agreed with those thoughts and would have asked my date for a rain check. But since I learned Step 4, "Train Your Thoughts" as well as the importance of Step 7, "Keep Your Commitments," I was armed with the tools to stay on the right course. I kept those commitments, and they have led me to some great new relationships with highly successful, talented, and intelligent entrepreneurs whom I enjoy brainstorming with to this day.

When you consider others and keep your commitments to them, you are exchanging healthy energy with the universe that will help you receive great rewards in the long run.

Keep Your Commitment to Yourself

Sometimes the most challenging commitments to keep are the ones we make with ourselves. It is so easy to let ourselves off the hook when we don't feel like doing something that we had intended to do. Once again, which habit do you want to build? Putting something off so that any time you have an intention, your likelihood of completing the task is 50/50? Or do you want to build the habit of completing things so that every time you set a goal, your natural inclination is to achieve it? One of the best ways to keep your commitments to yourself is to make sure you don't bite off more than you can chew.

For example, when this book was more than halfway completed, I set a goal of having my book done and ready to send to the editors in eight weeks. While that goal was perfectly doable, it did NOT happen. What I needed to do to ensure my success was to break it down into manageable pieces. Unfortunately, I did not do that. Every time I sat down to work on the book, I would think, *"I need to finish my book. I need to finish my book."* It was overwhelming and often led to writer's block. So June of 2014 came and went without me accomplishing that goal.

Afterward, I followed my own advice and broke it down. I started telling myself, *"I will work on my book for one hour today."* That was a much more manageable step, and I would find that my thoughts would flow so freely that often, when I finished writing for that day, I discovered that I had written well beyond the one hour to which I had committed.

What are some of the commitments you've made to yourself lately? Maybe you've committed to donate a certain number of pounds in order to achieve your ideal weight. Donating weight is a goal that also needs to be broken down in order for you to have the greatest chance of keeping your commitment. Perhaps you could start with something such as "Today I will eat three different colors of produce and get five minutes of exercise." The brain can manage that task much more efficiently than it can the task of letting go of unwanted pounds. So I invite you to take a look at the commitments you have made to yourself. It helps to write them down. "Don't just think it. **Ink it.**"[24] Next, you'll want to look at your list of commitments and write down some simple, manageable tasks you could take that will lead you to that end goal. By doing this activity, you will be more likely to keep your commitment and stay on course.

> *"You can't build a reputation on what you're going to do."*
> —Henry Ford

So make your list of what is nonnegotiable in your life and stick to it. Make time for God, always consider others, and stay true to you! Do what you *say* you're going to do and watch how beautifully the world responds.

Afterword

Remember the cocktail party that I spoke about at the beginning of this book? If you'll recall, shortly before that party, I started receiving thoughts and ideas about the props I could bring with me to represent who I would be in five years. One of the props was a plastic pretend medal I had purchased that said "WINNER" on it. It was attached to a red, white, and blue ribbon so you could wear it around your neck. My intention for this prop was to have it represent a finisher's medal, and five months later, I completed my first half marathon. About 14 months after that, Fit, Fab & Lean˚, Inc. was officially in business.

Another prop I prepared for that party was a picture book filled with photos of some famous speakers I had met in my life. I was going to use this picture book to say, "These are some of the folks with whom I have had the honor of sharing the stage during my travels around the world as an inspirational speaker." I'd like to tell you that I have made that a reality as well; however, I have not *yet* shared the stage with Oprah, John Maxwell, Les Brown, or James Malinchak. I'm pretty sure they'll be calling soon, though.

And my final prop was a book. I created a pretend cover of what I thought my first book cover might look like. I placed it over a real paperback book from my library. I brought it with me to the party, and I was going to say, "I am a best-selling author." I will tell you that I *did* share this particular prop with some of the speakers at that event. And I even asked them to sign *my first best-selling book*. One of them, author Simon T. Bailey, wrote, "Valerie, Thank you for sharing your best seller with me. You are BRILLIANT!" This final prop is what led to the book you are holding in your hands today.

I want to thank you from the top of my heart (it's way bigger than the bottom) for allowing me to share my experience with you. I invite you to share this book with your loved ones so that during those times when they find themselves in a valley, they too will be equipped with the right steps to climb back to the top.

I invite you to implement these seven easy steps to break you free:

Use today.
Navigate your course.
Start making yourself more visible.
Train your thoughts.
Unleash your passion.
Celebrate something each day.
Keep your commitments.

And step into your
B.L.I.S.S.—*Because Life Is So Spectacular.*
And now is the time to enjoy it.

Appendix

Low-Energy Words and Their Possible High-Energy Counterparts Based on Dr. Yvonne Oswald's Book *Every Word Has Power*

Low-energy words/phrases	High-energy words/phrases
No problem	My pleasure
Don't worry	Have faith
Bad	Not good
If	When
Hope	Trust
Try	Intend to
Sick	Not well
But	And
Hard	Not easy
Difficult	Not easy or challenging
Can't wait (sends procrastination signal)	Looking forward to / I'm so excited

(continued)

Low-energy words/phrases	High-energy words/phrases
I don't have time (we all have the same 24 hours)	I choose to spend my time on other things
Failure	Great lesson / learning experience
Upset	Not happy
Angry	Twirly
I should exercise	I choose to _____ (run/walk, etc.)
You should/ought to	It would be a great idea to …
I'm sorry	I apologize / my apologies
Busy	Productive
To do list	Ta-da list / Victory list
Bucket List (things to do before you die)	Life List (things to do while you're alive)
Can't afford it	Not ready to make the investment
Poor	Not rich yet
Weight loss*	Donate or let go of weight
Diet**	Healthy eating plan

*Loss can instruct the unconscious mind to go and find it.

**Diet contains the word *die* and sends that signal to your unconscious mind. Because its job is to keep you alive, it will then set out not only to make you hungry but also to send you to the fridge to bring you lots of food so that you don't die.

Notes

1. A "come as you will be in 5 years" party is a concept from the book *The Success Principles* by Jack Canfield (New York: Harper, 2005, 93–97).
2. "Act as if . . ." is success principle 12 in *The Success Principles* (90–97).
3. The roots of the words *decision* and *incision* are according to Membean.com and can be found at http://ffal.us/1GolKzH.
4. Steve Jobs's 2005 commencement speech at Stanford University can be seen here http://ffal.us/SJHowToLiveBeforeYouDie.
5. This is a famous quote by James Dewar, Scottish chemist and physicist.
6. "How Writing by Hand Makes Kids Smarter" by *The Week* staff, October 6, 2010, available at http://ffal.us/1xPMqSA.
7. "How Handwriting Trains the Brain" by Gwendolyn Bounds, October 5, 2010, available at http://ffal.us/156Tw9B.

8. These three questions were inspired by a speech I heard in 2011 given by author Simon T. Bailey, who asked the audience three very similar questions. The questions were great thought starters for me on my journey to getting unstuck.
9. The definition of *inspire* is according to The Free Dictionary at http://ffal.us/1yW8JUI.
10. This is according to Wikipedia and can be found on http://en.wikipedia.org/wiki/Nick_Vujicic.
11. This passage is from *Think and Grow Rich* by Napoleon Hill.
12. This is a famous quote by Joel Weldon, Hall of Fame speaker.
13. This is a famous quote by Zig Ziglar, author and motivational speaker.
14. This is a famous quote by Jackie Robinson, baseball player.
15. This is a famous quote by Abraham Lincoln, the 16th president of the United States.
16. This is according to the Laboratory of Neuro Imaging (LONI) at the University of Southern California, which studies the brain.
17. The definition of *psychoneuroimmunology* is according to *Merriam-Webster's Dictionary*, which can be found at http://ffal.us/1zvUDZx.
18. This is taken from the book *Ageless Body, Timeless Mind* by Deepak Chopra, part one, "The Land Where No One Is Old."
19. Ibid., page 17.
20. *Every Word has Power* (New York: Atria, 2008), Yvonne Oswald, pages 42–43.
21. Ibid., Yvonne Oswald, pages 11–12.
22. Ibid., Yvonne Oswald, pages 11–12.
23. Ibid., Yvonne Oswald, page 12.
24. The definition of *passion* is according to *Merriam-Webster's Dictionary*, which can be found at http://ffal.us/1rXcA4C.

25. "What Are Endorphins?" by Elizabeth Quinn, *About.com*, May 27, 2014, available at http://ffal.us/1pf8jYy.
26. "Exercise and Depression" by WebMD, 2014, available at http://ffal.us/1xTPs8s.
27. This is a famous quote by author Mark Victor Hansen.

Recommended Resources

Ageless Body, Timeless Mind by Deepak Chopra
The Alchemist by Paulo Coelho
Awaken the Giant Within by Tony Robbins
The Difference Maker by John Maxwell
The Encore Effect by Mark Sanborn
Everyone Communicates Few Connect by John Maxwell
Everything You Need to Know to Feel Go(O)D by Candace Perk
Every Word Has Power by Yvonne Oswald
The Four Agreements by Don Miguel Ruiz
The Fred Factor by Mark Sanborn
Have I Ever Told You You're My Favorite by Maryann Ehmann
Jesus Calling by Sarah Young
Live Your Best Life by Joel Osteen
The Power of Positive Thinking by Norman Vincent Peale
Rich Dad Poor Dad by Robert Kiyosaki

The Secret by Rhonda Byrne

Secrets of the Millionaire Mind by T. Harv Eker

Seven Prayers That Will Change Your Life Forever by Stormie Omartian

A Simple Act of Gratitude by John Kralik

Success Is Not an Accident by Tommy Newberry

The Success Principles by Jack Canfield

Think and Grow Rich by Napoleon Hill

UNSTUCK! by Valerie Brunnberg

www.ingramcontent.com/pod-product-compliance
Lightning Source LLC
Chambersburg PA
CBHW060501080526
44584CB00015B/1515